This book is a presentation of Weekly Reader
Books. Weekly Reader Books offers book
clubs for children from preschool through high
school. For further information write to:
WEEKLY READER BOOKS, 4343 Equity Drive,
Columbus, Ohio 43228

This edition is published by arrangement
with Checkerboard Press.

Weekly Reader is a federally registered trademark
of Field Publications.

WEEKLY READER BOOKS presents

Why Does It Thunder and Lightning?

A **Just Ask**™ Book

Hi, my name is Christopher!

by Chris Arvetis
and Carole Palmer

illustrated by
James Buckley

FIELD PUBLICATIONS
MIDDLETOWN, CT.

What a storm!
The lightning lights
up the sky.
The thunder can be
heard all around.
I wonder —
what makes lightning
and thunder?

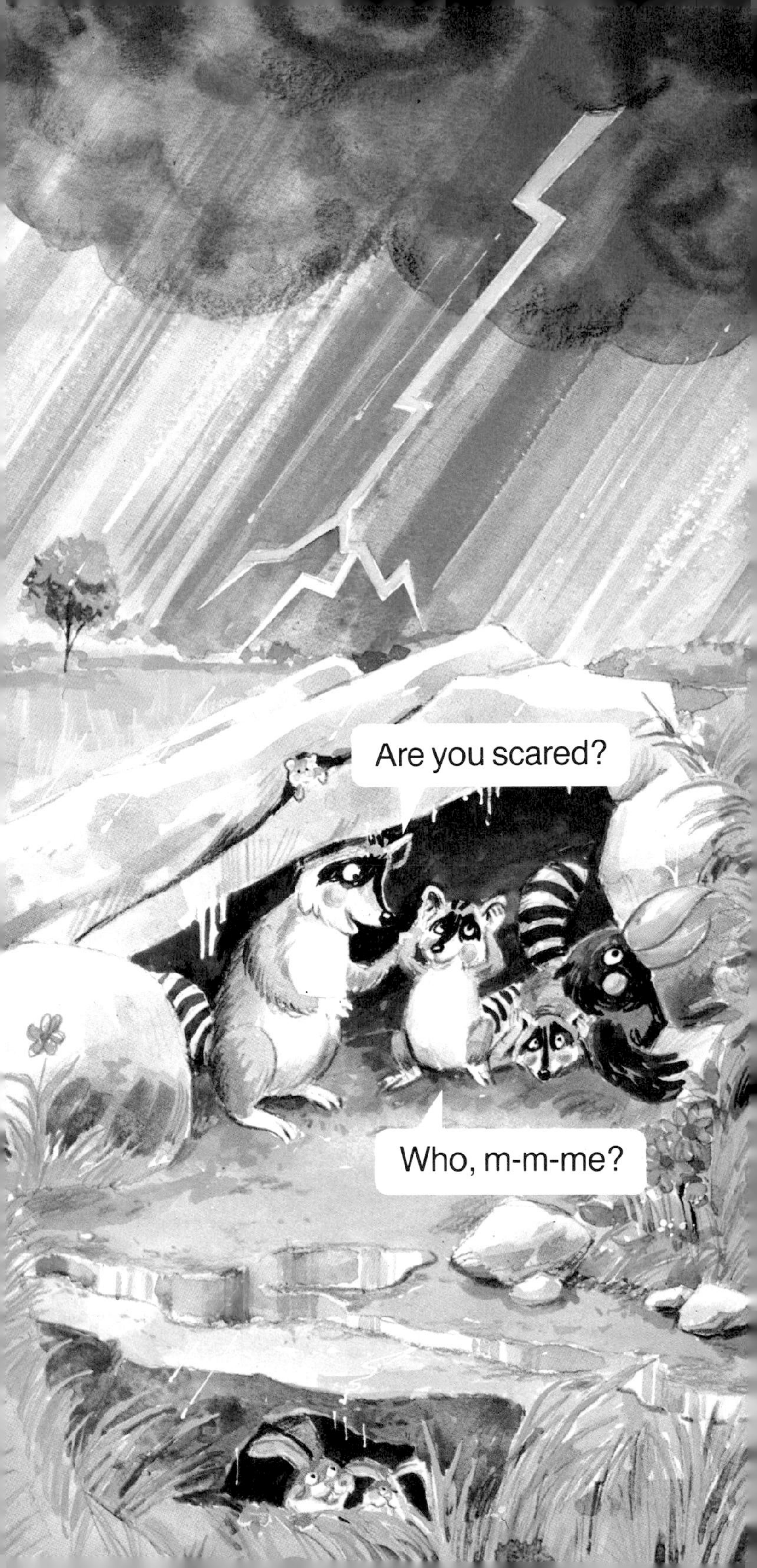
Are you scared?
Who, m-m-me?

I bet Raccoon knows.
I'll go and ask her.
Hi, my friend!
Can you tell me—
what makes lightning
and thunder?

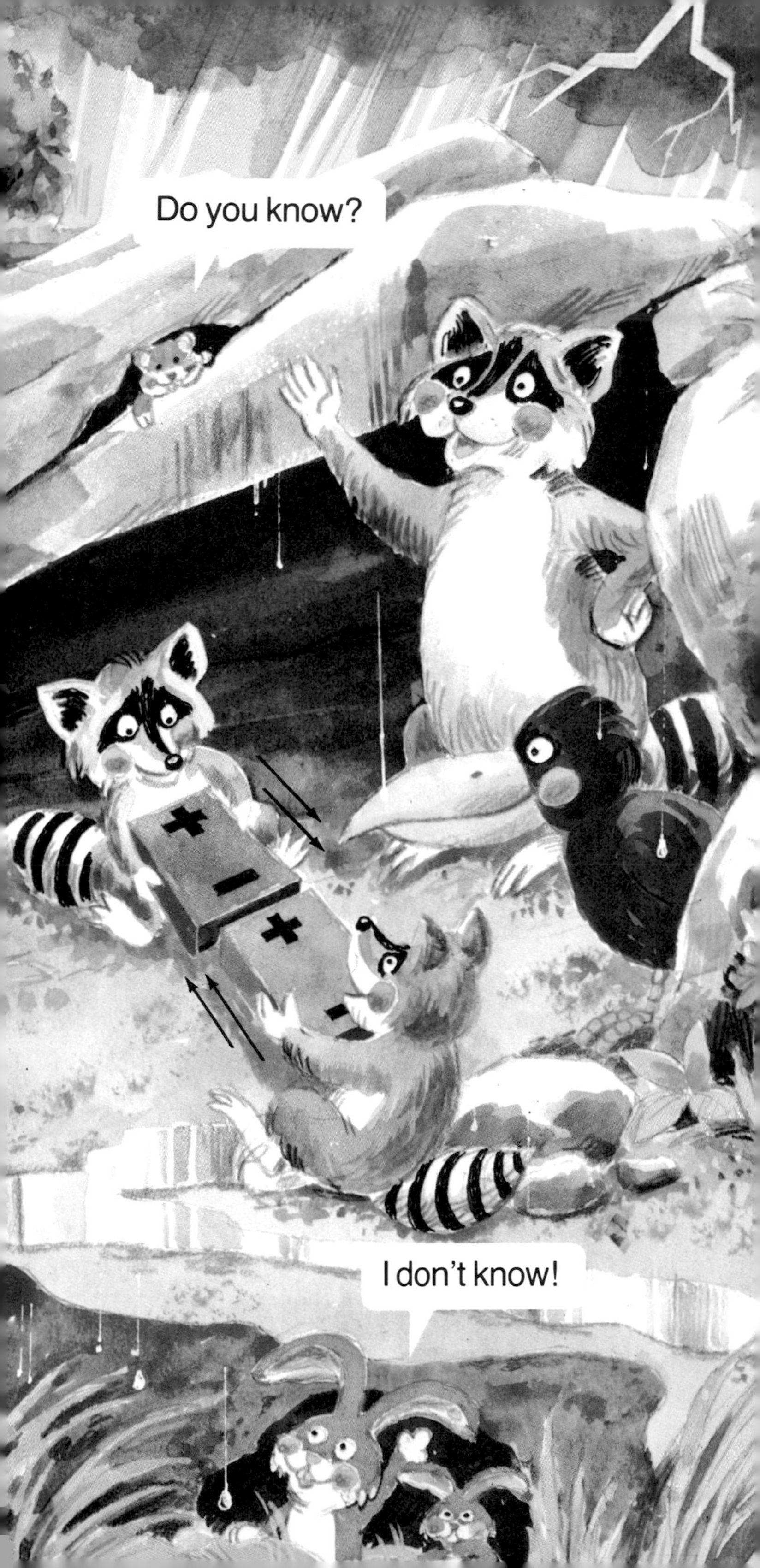
Do you know?
+
-
+
-
I don't know!

Christopher, you ask the hardest questions.
Let's start with lightning.
It is caused by electricity.
We can't see electricity, but we can use these magnets to learn about it.

Look at the magnets.

Each one has a positive + side and a negative − side.

When we put this magnet next to the other, the magnets come together.

That's because the + side of one magnet attracts the − side of the other.

Opposites attract.

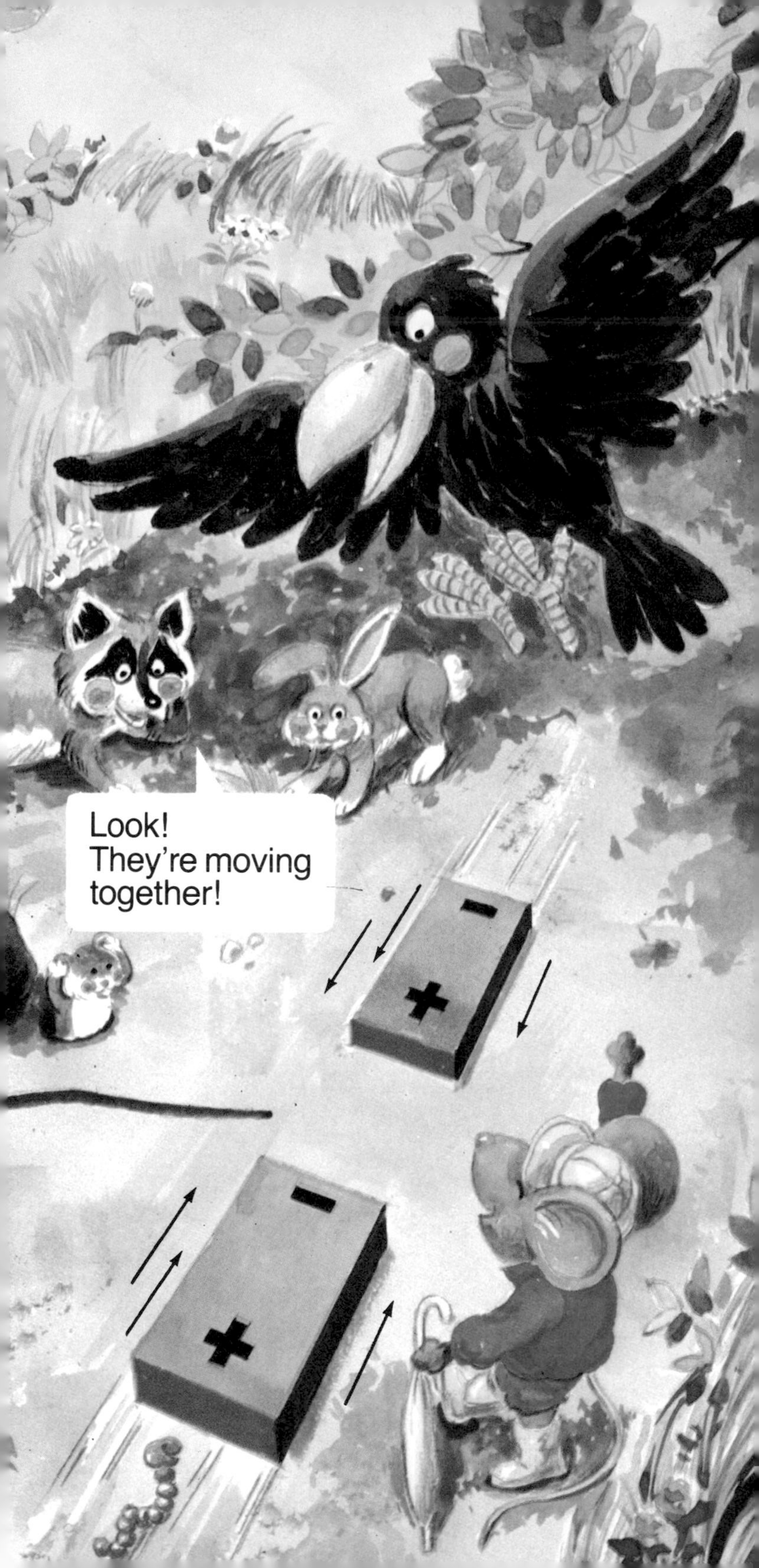
Look!
They're moving together!
-
+
-
+

Let's turn one of the
magnets around.
When we use the other end,
the two magnets push apart.
That is because the sides of the
magnets with the same sign
do NOT attract.

Now that you know a little about positive and negative, let's see what they have to do with electricity.

You and Crow can go up and look at that storm cloud.

Look at the cloud.

A cloud is made up of many,
many drops of water.

When the drops get big and
heavy, they fall toward
the earth as rain.

Some of the drops have
a positive + charge
of electricity.

Some of them have
a negative − charge.

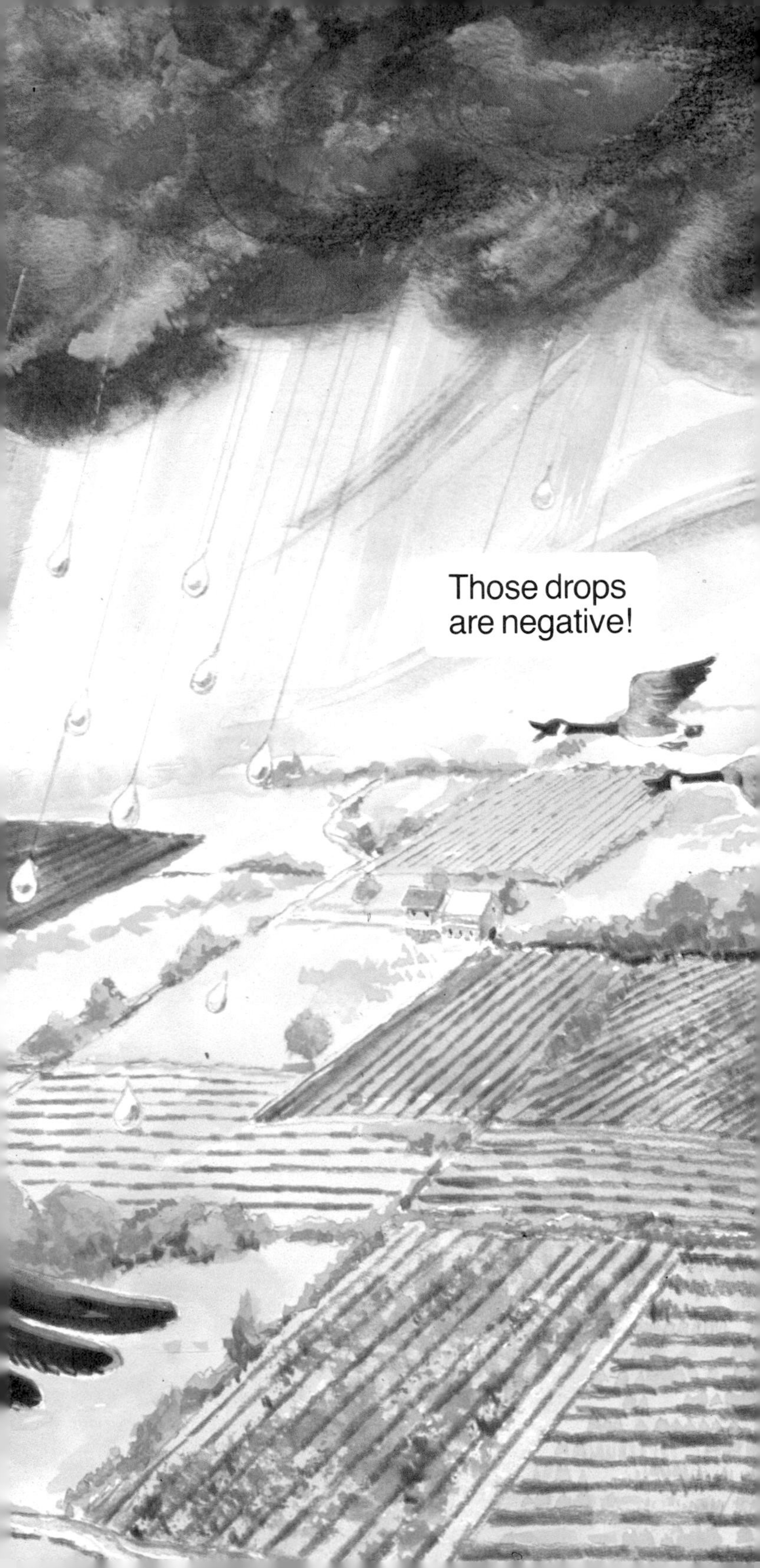
Those drops
are negative!

Let's look inside the cloud.

When a group of drops with a positive charge comes near a group with a negative charge, a large electrical spark is caused.

Then we see a flash of lightning jump between the two groups of drops.

It's just like the magnets—opposites attract.

This same thing can happen between two different clouds that come near each other.

If a group of drops in one cloud has a positive charge and a group in the other cloud has a negative charge, lightning can jump between the clouds!

Sometimes lightning
jumps from a storm cloud
to the ground.

The earth and a group
of drops in the cloud
attract each other
because they have
opposite charges.

Lightning is powerful and,
at times, very dangerous.

Look!
It hit that tree, and now
the tree is burning!

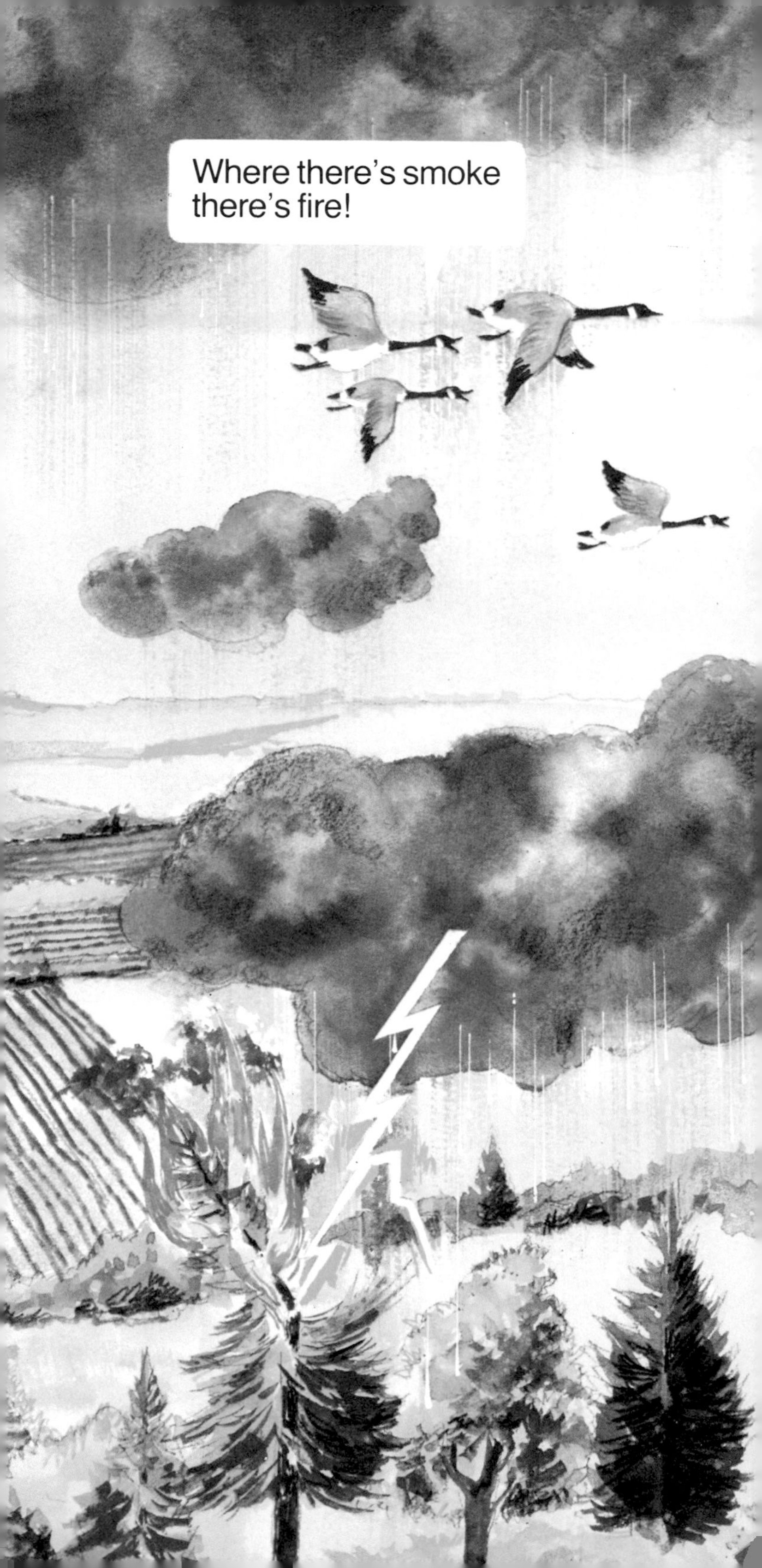
Where there's smoke there's fire!

Now I know about lightning.
But what about thunder?
All that booming and crackling
frightens me.

Thunder is just a lot of noise.
It's nothing to be afraid of.
But Raccoon can explain
that better than I can.

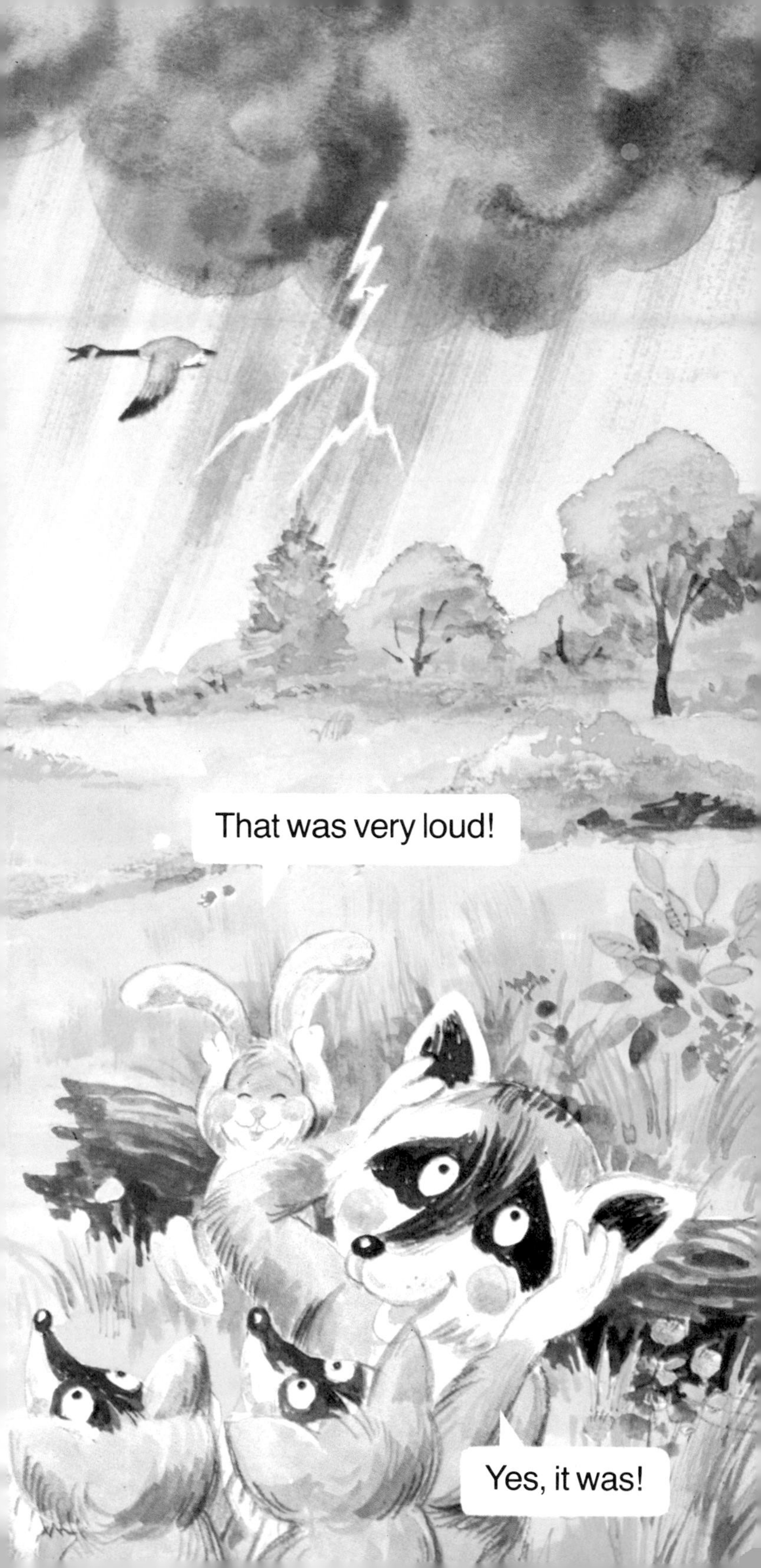
That was very loud!
Yes, it was!

Air is made up of tiny parts
called molecules.

Say MOL-E-CULES.

When lightning flashes,
it gives off a lot of heat.

This heat makes the
molecules start to
move and bounce.

MOL-E-CULES!

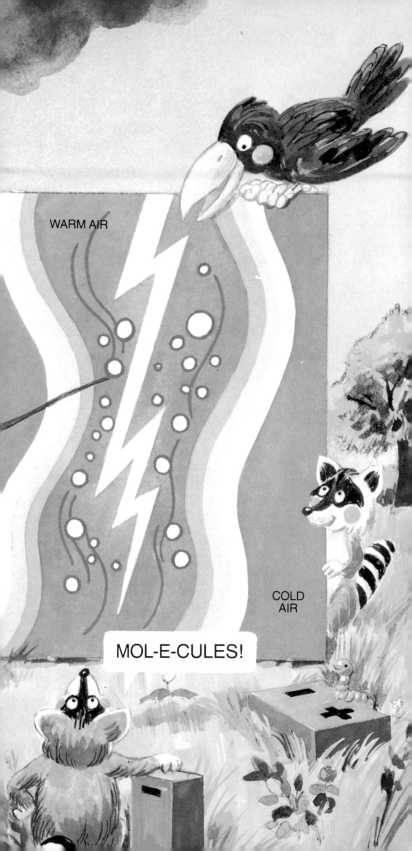

Soon the heated molecules bump into molecules of cold air and make a big air wave.

This wave is the sound of thunder we hear after we see a flash of lightning!

So thunder is just a lot of harmless noise.

Let's review what we know.
The drops of water in a
cloud can have a positive
or a negative charge.

When two opposite charges
come near each other, a
large spark of electricity
happens and we see
a flash of lightning!

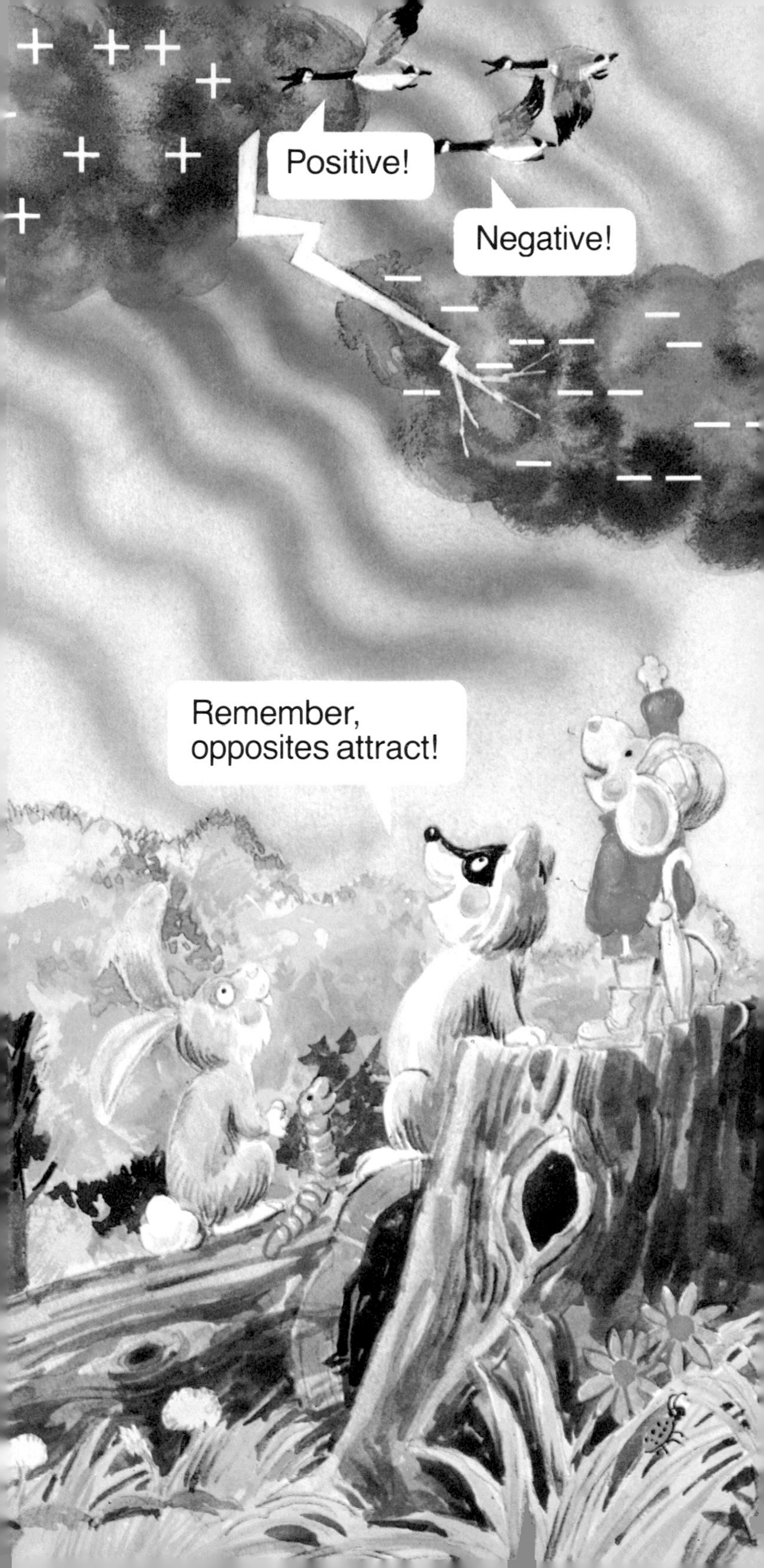
Positive!
Negative!
Remember, opposites attract!

As the lightning heats the air, the molecules bounce together and make a great air wave— the sound of thunder!